ARTS AND CRAFTS

TEXTILES AND
INTERIORS

ARTS AND CRAFTS
TEXTILES AND INTERIORS

Grange
BOOKS

A QUANTUM BOOK

Published by Grange Books
an imprint of Grange Books Plc
The Grange
Kingsnorth Industrial Estate
Hoo, nr. Rochester
Kent ME3 9ND

1-84013-266-3

This book is produced by
Quantum Books Ltd
6 Blundell Street
London N7 9BH

Project Manager: Rebecca Kingsley
Project Editor: Judith Millidge
Designer: Wayne Humphries
Editor: Clare Haworth-Maden

The material in this publication previously appeared in
The Arts and Crafts Movement, William Morris

QUMACTW
Set in Times
Reproduced in Singapore by Eray Scan (Pte) Ltd
Printed in Singapore by Star Standard Industries (Pte) Ltd

CONTENTS

THE ARTS AND CRAFTS
PHILOSOPHY

The Arts and Crafts Movement developed in England as a protest against the character of mid-Victorian manufactured products and slowly evolved during the period between 1850 and 1920 into an international campaign for design reform that affected all aspects of the environment, from architecture and gardens to interior furnishings, finishing materials and fittings. Throughout its life span, its supporters argued that design affects society – that the character of the living and working environment moulds the character of the individual.

These were devout reformers who feared that mid-nineteenth-century design had gone astray. They not only condemned the shoddy workmanship, indiscriminate use of materials, inefficient forms and elaborate ornamentation that characterised most mid-Victorian manufactured products, but believed that such products had a deleterious effect upon society. By initiating a programme of reform, they hoped to improve the quality of design and thus to strengthen the character of the individual and of society as a whole. To achieve their goal, they strove to ensure that traditional methods of handcraftsmanship would survive, despite competition with machine production, to ameliorate the working conditions of artisans and craftsmen and to encourage artistic collaboration among workers. Their intention was to improve the quality of life for everyone by restoring integrity to the objects common to daily living.

INTERNATIONAL EXHIBITIONS

The clamour for design reform had begun largely in reaction to the falling standards of taste as exemplified by products shown at international exhibitions. These enormous world fairs, which took place regularly throughout the nineteenth century, were six-monthly celebrations of industrial technology and of the potential of the machine. Beginning with the Great Exhibition of 1851, which was held in London, they stood as testimonies to the changing aesthetic and technical standards of an era.

Products ranged from mass-produced, everyday wares to one-of-a-kind presentation pieces. Those in the former category often introduced newly developed materials or patented mechanisms; those in the latter were remarkable primarily for their size, complexity and cost or investment of labour. Stylistically, most demonstrated a reliance upon the past, their retrospective appearance contradicting the fact that they embodied the latest developments in technology.

THE 'MACHINE AGE' CONDEMNED

Although such fairs were intended to glorify the accomplishments of the 'machine age', to design reformers they invited more criticism than approbation. Surveying the manufactured products on display, many disapproved not only of what was being made, but also of how it was made, and with a degree of enthusiasm that belied their relatively small numbers they set about changing both.

They questioned whether it was appropriate to utilise new materials and processes in order to create elaborate works that recalled, with

Opposite: New machinery on show at the 1851 Great Exhibition in London.

Below: A stoneware vase by Adrien-Pierre Dalpyrat, with ormolu mounts by Keller, exhibited at the Paris Exhibition of 1900.

varying degrees of accuracy, the historical styles of the past. They pondered the relative merits of machine production as it affected form, ornament and finish. They weighed up the manner in which materials were selected and used. And they objected to the fact that most goods were manufactured in stages, using a so-called 'division of labour'.

The comprehensive vision of the independent pre-'machine age' craftsman, true or false, had been replaced by the limited perspective of the machine operator who laboured in relative isolation. Designers seldom had contact any longer with the craftsmen who implemented their ideas and few workers ever saw the finished product. Manufacturers had little exposure to the consumers who used their wares and could not therefore assess their reactions. What had once been an integrated, cyclical process had become segregated and linear and the resulting lack of communication caused standards of design and construction to deteriorate.

Reformers hoped to improve design by restoring conditions that they believed had been typical before the Industrial Revolution. They addressed such issues as the training, education and working conditions of the designer or craftsman; the aesthetic or technical attributes of the end product; and the manner in which products became available to the public. In addition, they considered the effect which products common to daily living had upon the user's environment and the appropriateness of the products for its intended purpose. Whether or not they were interested

Right: Luke Fildes, Applicants for Admission to a Casual Labour Ward, *oil on canvas, 1874.*

in changing every stage of the design process, all of the reformers hoped for essentially the same outcome: the restoration of dignity to the maker; integrity to the product; discrimination to the user; and artistic co-operation throughout the design process.

THE ARTS AND CRAFTS PHILOSOPHY

Although the questionable standards of mid-Victorian manufactured products undoubtedly justified the need for reform, the ideals of English design reformers would never have gained international acceptance without the benefit of a strong and widely publicised philosophical argument. This was propounded chiefly by three ardent advocates, A W N Pugin, John Ruskin and William Morris, who, by word and deed, spread the message not only throughout Britain but also throughout the industrialised world.

A W N PUGIN

The design reformer's major premise, that the character of the living and working environment moulds the character of the individual, evolved from a related idea promulgated by Pugin in the 1830s. A designer, writer and the son of a French *émigré* architect, Pugin believed that the character of a nation was expressed by its architecture and applied arts. He recommended that English architects and designers should abandon their allegiance to Graeco-Roman models in favour of Gothic examples from the late Middle Ages, the greater suitability of the latter, he argued, stemming from its association with a Christian rather than a pagan culture. He made this case passionately in such influential books as *Contrasts* and *The True Principles of Pointed or Christian Architecture*.

As well as their symbolic appropriateness,

Right: A maiolica plate designed by A W N Pugin, c. 1850. Pugin designed both buildings and their contents.

Far right: Wallpaper with Tudor rose and portcullis, with the initials of Queen Victoria, designed by Pugin for the Houses of Parliament.

Below: The church of All Saints, Leek, Staffordshire, by Gerald Horsley. Pen and watercolour, 1891.

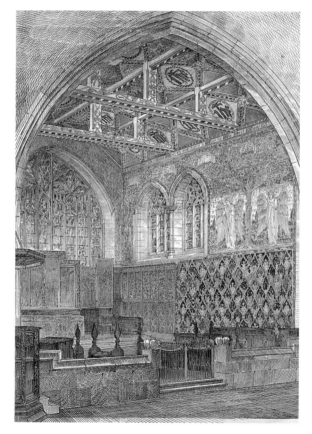

Pugin maintained that Gothic and other styles from the Middle Ages were superior for their integrity. He admired the functional nature of the plan, the expressive quality of the façade and the integration of structure and ornament that characterised medieval architecture. He suggested that such features were absent from contemporary British architecture and he recommended that architects and designers could learn valuable lessons by studying the work of their medieval predecessors. 'There should be no features about a building which are not necessary for convenience, construction or propriety', he wrote.

With a similarly pragmatic attitude, he stated: 'All ornaments should consist of enrichment of the essential construction of the building', advocating a degree of decorative restraint. His belief in the moral and aesthetic superiority of the Gothic style inspired a generation of architects and designers (many of whom trained supporters of the Arts and Crafts Movement) and stimulated enthusiasm for the Gothic Revival style in Britain and abroad.

JOHN RUSKIN

Like Pugin, John Ruskin, architectural critic and first Slade professor at Oxford (1868), equated the character of the nation with that of its architecture. He believed that the nature of contemporary British architecture would improve if it were designed to express qualities exemplified by the Romanesque and Gothic styles. In *The Seven Lamps of Architecture* (1849), he identified those qualities as Sacrifice, Truth, Power, Beauty, Life, Memory and Obedience and explained how each might be conveyed by form, ornament or construction.

In *The Seven Lamps of Architecture*, Ruskin provided aesthetic recommendations, arguing

Below: A portrait of John Ruskin by T B Wirgman.

Bottom: A photograph of John Ruskin, the historian, educator and writer.

in favour of simplified massing (Power), naturalistic ornamentation (Beauty), historicism of style (Obedience) and an honest use of materials (Truth). He also addressed the issue of construction, demonstrating that he was as concerned with the process of building as with the finished product. He suggested that architecture must reflect the thoughtfulness and feeling of each individual involved in its construction. 'I believe the right question to ask, respecting all ornament,' he wrote in 'The Lamp of Life', 'is simply this: Was it done with enjoyment . . . was the carver happy while he was about it?'

Ruskin continued to explore this theme in *The Stones of Venice* (1851–53), an influential work in three volumes that provided an in-depth analysis of Venetian architecture from the Middle Ages. In one section, an essay entitled 'On the Nature of Gothic', Ruskin summarised the qualities that gave medieval architecture its distinctive character. These included Rudeness (imperfection or lack of precision), Changefulness (variety, asymmetry and random placement of elements), Naturalism (truthfulness or realism as opposed to conventionalisation), Grotesqueness (delight in the fantastic), Rigidity (conveyed by sprightly or energetic forms and ornament) and lastly Redundance (achieved through the repetition of ornament). He viewed each quality as an extension of the craftsman's personality and believed that each was essential to achieving an architecture of character.

As long as the 'division of labour' degraded the 'operative [or worker] into a machine',

Right: The design by William Burges for St Mary's, Alford-cum-Studley, Yorkshire, c. 1872. Watercolour by Axel Naig.

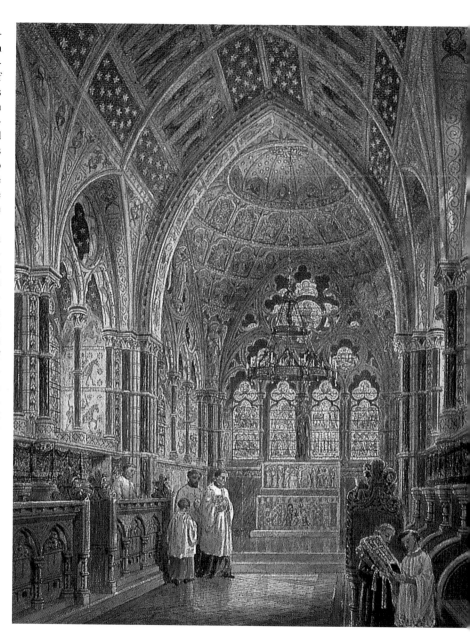

architecture would fail to achieve the qualities of medieval architects. He advocated changing the design process to foster an environment of 'healthy and ennobling labour'. To achieve such an atmosphere, he proposed 'three broad and simple rules' to be applied by architects, designers and manufacturers.

1 Never encourage the manufacture of an article not absolutely necessary in the production of which Invention has no share.
2 Never demand an exact finish for its own sake, but only for some practical or noble end.
3 Never encourage imitation or copying of any kind, except for the sake of preserving records of great works.

Without dictating a specific formula for design reform, Ruskin established an ideal, and for the next 70 years that ideal, as set forth in 'On the Nature of Gothic', continued to inspire reformers.

WILLIAM MORRIS

The leader among these was William Morris, who began to study at Oxford in 1853, two years after the Great Exhibition in London and in the year in which 'On the Nature of Gothic' first appeared. As a student, Morris developed a profound affection for the culture of the Middle Ages, stimulated by his familiarity with Ruskin's works, his appreciation of Oxford's medieval architecture and his travels in France to the cathedral cities of Amiens, Beauvais and Chartres. His sensitivity to his surroundings was strengthened by a two-year apprenticeship in the Oxford office of

Below left: William Morris pictured when at Oxford, aged 23.

Below right: A photograph of Edward Burne-Jones and William Morris by Hollyer, taken in about 1890.

the Gothic Revival architect George Edmund Street. Although he abandoned architecture to take up painting, the time that Morris spent in Street's office was invaluable, for it was there that he developed a life-long friendship with the senior clerk, Philip Webb, whom he had met at Oxford.

This friendship was one of several fortuitous connections made by Morris at Oxford. While there, he also met a fellow painter, Edmund Burne-Jones, and still another painter and poet, Dante Gabriel Rossetti, both of whom, with him, were later to be members of the Pre-Raphaelite Brotherhood. Like Webb, they shared Morris' passion for the culture of the Middle Ages. They were inspired not only by its architecture, art and craft, but also by the artistic co-operation which had fostered their creation.

RED HOUSE

The commitment of these friends to the artisanry and atmosphere of the Middle Ages was tangibly expressed in Red House, the marital home designed by Webb for Morris and his bride, Jane Burden. The house is as significant for the manner in which it was built and furnished as for its warm and unassuming appearance. Proudly handcrafted by workers involved throughout the building process, it was in essence a communal labour of love to which Morris' entire circle of artistic friends contributed. A unified whole, related from large scale to small, from site to hardware and from

Above right: Red House, Bexley Heath, Kent, designed by Philip Webb for William Morris and his bride.

Right: A caricature by Rossetti, Morris Presenting an Engagement Ring to Jane.

exterior to interior, it has become a monument of the Arts and Crafts Movement, not so much for what it is but for what it symbolises.

MORRIS, MARSHALL, FAULKNER & CO

The collaborative effort manifest in Red House prompted the formation in 1861 of Morris, Marshall, Faulkner & Co, 'Fine Art Workmen in Painting, Carving, Furniture and the Metals'. The company specialised in ecclesiastical and residential commissions and its reputation flourished as the result of exposure at various international exhibitions. It was organised somewhat in the manner of a medieval guild; its members, including Burne-Jones, Webb, Rossetti and Ford Madox Brown, developed their designs, carried them through to completion, collaborated with one another and dealt closely with clients, deriving satisfaction all the while from their work process and its outcome.

In 1875, Morris assumed full responsibility for the firm, abbreviating its name to Morris & Co. The enterprise produced a wide range of interior furnishings, finishing materials and fittings and provided advice regarding interior decoration. Among Morris' many personal responsibilities during the 1870s, 1880s and 1890s were the design and production of over 600 chintzes, woven textiles and hand-blocked wallpapers, a task that involved his researching dyes, weaves and printing techniques. As designer, craftsman and entrepreneur, his goal was ambitious: to provide a tasteful and affordable alternative to the products of the Industrial Revolution, which he condemned as 'masses of sordidness, filth and squalor, embroidered with patches of pompous and vulgar hideousness'.

Morris' considerable talents extended to poetry, printing, preservation, writing and

Top: 'Snakeshead' printed cotton, 1876, designed by William Morris and one of his own favourites.

Above: Linoleum designed by William Morris in 1875, available in two colourways. This was Morris' only design for this medium, although linoleum was very popular at the time.

politics. In his later years, he devoted much of his time and energy to the cause of social reform, formally allying himself to socialism in 1883. At the Kelmscott Press, which he operated from 1891 to his death in 1896, he hand-printed Utopian polemics, such as his novel *News from Nowhere*. 'What business have we with art at all', he often asked, 'if we cannot all share it?' This query prompted scores of his followers to embrace socialism with enthusiasm, convinced that design reform was impossible to achieve unless preceded by social, political and economic changes.

Throughout his career, Morris struggled to reconcile his artistic ideals with his political inclinations. His commitment to the creation of products that reflected the highest standards of design and construction seemed constantly at odds with his desire to produce them at a cost that middle-class consumers could afford. His dedication to utilising the aesthetic and technical skills of craftsmen to their fullest potential, in a Ruskinian atmosphere of 'healthy and ennobling labour', conflicted with the necessity of using machine production wherever possible to eliminate the drudgery of certain tasks and to reduce production costs. It was a dilemma that he never fully resolved while director of Morris & Co, and it continued to plague his followers in the years to come.

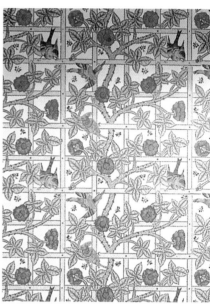

Top left: 'Dove and Rose' woven silk and wool double cloth, designed by William Morris in 1879.

Top right: 'Trellis' wallpaper by William Morris, 1864.

Right: 'The Orchard Tapestry' by William Morris, 1890.

PRACTITIONERS AND DISSEMINATION

Although Morris & Co may have been only a qualified success from an economic standpoint, it nevertheless served as a testimony to the merits of artistic co-operation. It inspired a host of imitators throughout England, in both urban and rural locations, where small groups of architects, designers, craftsmen and critics banded together in organisations dedicated to design reform.

Among these were the Century Guild, founded in 1882 by the architect Arthur Heygate Mackmurdo; the Art Workers' Guild, formed in 1884 by pupils of the architect Richard Norman Shaw and which still exists; and the Guild of Handicraft, organised in 1888 by the architect Charles Robert Ashbee.

Many of them were patterned on medieval guilds, and, as such, established certain aesthetic and technical standards for their supporters, who were sometimes ranked according to their level of expertise in a particular craft. Some groups assumed educational roles, offering lectures, workshops and classes. Most held regular exhibitions to promote the work of members and to elevate public taste. The most venerable of these was the Arts and Crafts Exhibition Society, which used the name suggested by the bookbinder T J Cobden-Sanderson. During the life span of the Arts and Crafts Movement, similar guilds and societies developed throughout Britain, Europe and the United States, and were the primary means by which the ideals of the movement were disseminated.

Previous page: 'Artichoke' embroidered hanging, in crewel wools on a linen ground, by William Morris, 1877.

Left: A tile panel designed by Edward Burne-Jones, probably painted by Lucy or Kate Faulkner in around 1861.

THE CENTURY GUILD

A pupil in John Ruskin's Oxford drawing class and a companion on Ruskin's visits to Italy, Mackmurdo established the Century Guild on the advice of his teacher in 1882. In the following year, the Century Guild's workshops were opened in partnership with Selwyn Image, who worked in several media. Other members of the guild included the potter William De Morgan, the designer Heywood Sumner, the sculptor Benjamin Creswick, the textile designer and metalworker H P Horne and the metalworker Clement Heaton. Mackmurdo himself had trained as an architect but had, in addition, attempted to learn several crafts, including brasswork, embroidery and cabinetmaking.

The purpose of the Century Guild was to accommodate craftsmen active in a number of *métiers* and to unite the traditionally separate disciplines of architecture, interior design and decoration. It also aimed to raise the status of such crafts as building, fabric design, pottery and metalworking in order that they might take their place alongside the professionally respectable 'fine' arts.

Unlike the many medievalists associated with the Arts and Crafts Movement, Mackmurdo admired Italian Renaissance and even Baroque architecture and used the styles in his designs for several houses, including his own, Great Ruffins. The furniture produced by the guild was equally eclectic, ranging from

Right: A poster designed by Arthur Heygate Mackmurdo. Mackmurdo's work is dichotomous in character, at times angular and pragmatic, and at other times curvilinear and highly ornamental. Thus he was equally influential upon practitioners of Arts and Crafts and Art Nouveau.

the restrained and utilitarian to a style of decoration that anticipated the asymmetrical arabesques of the Aesthetic Movement and Art Nouveau. The guild was eventually dissolved in 1888.

THE ART WORKERS' GUILD

Selwyn Image was later active in another fraternity, the Art Workers' Guild. The guild was established in 1884 and was, in part, formed from a group of young architects employed in the architect Richard Norman Shaw's practice, among them William Richard Lethaby, Gerald Horsley, Ernest Newton, E S Prior and Mervyn Macartney. In 1884 Shaw's assistants merged with a group of writers, designers and theorists known as 'The Fifteen', led by Lewis Forman Day. The guild also included Walter Crane, John Sedding and Henry Holiday.

The Art Workers' Guild shared most of the concerns of other Arts and Crafts ventures: it sought a handcrafted, well-designed environment in which artists, architects and craftsmen would assume collective responsibility for buildings and their contents. It is, however, difficult to discern within the guild any clear sense of social purpose. It also seems to have kept a deliberately low profile.

THE GUILD OF HANDICRAFTS

Charles Robert Ashbee's Guild and School of Handicraft evolved from a Ruskin reading class held at Toynbee Hall in the East End of London under the direction of Ashbee, an associate of Morris and H M Hyndman. Whereas much of

Right: A silver salt cellar by C R Ashbee, made by the Guild of Handicraft, 1899–1900. The figure was probably worked by William Hardiman, Ashbee's chief modeller.

the produce of the Arts and Crafts Movement in the 1880s and 1890s had become increasingly eclectic in style and intention, often employing highly refined standards of craftsmanship and, in some instances, mechanised production, Ashbee's guild marked a distinct return to the Ruskinian and socialist principles that characterised the earlier work of the Arts and Crafts Movement.

Ashbee insisted that crafts should be self-taught, the skill of the craftsman gradually evolving as his familiarity with the medium increased. He deliberately recruited unskilled workers, educating them through the guild's classes. Labour within the guild's workshops was undivided, with each craftsman involved with the whole production process. Moreover, guild members were encouraged to work co-operatively, each one in appreciation of the strengths and weaknesses of his or her comrades. The work produced by the guild – particularly its metalwork and furniture – was simple in design.

In 1902 the fortunes of the guild changed after it moved from the East End to Chipping Camden in Gloucestershire. The countryside was a more appropriate setting for a craft fraternity and Ashbee established workshops in the run-down village with some 50 of his craftsmen and their families. By 1905, however, the guild's finances were looking precarious. A manager was appointed and attempts were made to raise capital from shareholders but the company eventually went into voluntary liquidation.

THE SPREAD OF ARTS AND CRAFTS IDEALS TO AMERICA

Contact between the British Arts and Crafts Movement and artists, architects and designers in the United States was, at first, limited. The

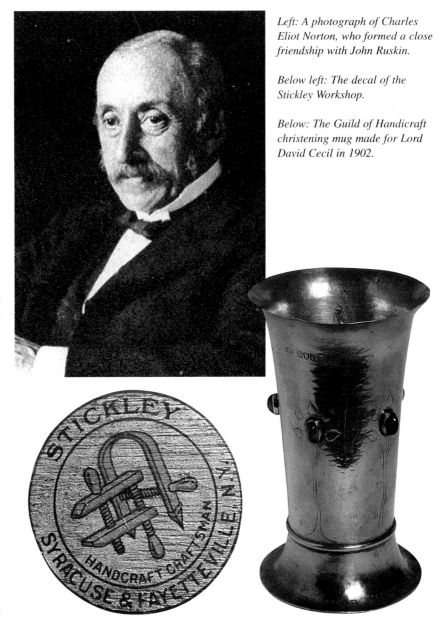

Left: A photograph of Charles Eliot Norton, who formed a close friendship with John Ruskin.

Below left: The decal of the Stickley Workshop.

Below: The Guild of Handicraft christening mug made for Lord David Cecil in 1902.

Above: The ethnographical room by Paul Hankar at the Exposition Internationale, Brussels, 1897.

Right: A Tiffany magnolia vase in silver, gold enamel and opals, which was exhibited at the World Columbian Exposition, Chicago, 1893.

work of Downing, Renwick and Jarves had been influenced by the revival of a Gothic style in Britain in the late nineteenth century and Ruskin's writing had been enthusiastically received by some American painters and critics. A more substantial grasp of the movement and its possible application to American culture did not really occur, however, until the Centennial Exposition held in Philadelphia in 1876.

Interest in the Arts and Crafts Movement in the United States was, for the most part, inspired by British contributors to the exhibition. Robert Norman Shaw exhibited several influential designs for buildings in the Queen Anne style, and equally important in the evolution of the American craft ideal were the other British Arts and Crafts exhibits. Jeffrey & Co – the firm that had printed Morris' first wallpapers – Fairfax Murray, Walter Crane and the Royal School of Art Needlework had all contributed to the exhibition. In addition, the work and, to a lesser extent, ideals of William Morris were becoming increasingly well known in the United States.

Below: A 'Tudric' tea set designed for Liberty & Co by Archibald Knox, 1904.

Below: An inkwell produced by the Wiener Werkstätte, which operated between 1903 and 1932.

THE SOCIETY OF ARTS AND CRAFTS

One of the oldest and most influential of the American groups was the Society of Arts and Crafts in Boston (SACB), which was established in 1897 and is still in operation. Modelled on the Arts and Crafts Exhibition Society, it began as a group of 71 architects, designers, craftsmen, philanthropists and connoisseurs, but within 20 years it had attracted an international membership of close to 1,000. The SACB provided an important philosophical connection between the British and American branches of the Arts and Crafts Movement, which was fostered by

Charles Eliot Norton, the first president of the SACB and a professor of fine arts at Harvard.

CHARLES ELIOT NORTON
While travelling in Europe between 1855 and 1857, Norton met John Ruskin, initiating a social and professional relationship that lasted for 45 years. Their friendship was fuelled by a variety of shared pleasures and mutual concerns, including respect for the culture of the Middle Ages, dedication to the preservation of ancient architecture and a belief in the restorative powers of the countryside. Their dismay at the encroachment of industrialisation upon rural areas paralleled their concern for the working conditions of the contemporary craftsman. To both, early Italian cathedrals were symbolic of a more joyous and productive age, and as a buffer against the assault of the present each surrounded himself with the artefacts and arts of the past.

Later, while living abroad with his wife and young family, Norton also came to know Morris, Rossetti, Burne-Jones and the essayist Thomas Carlyle. As a result of these contacts he became a life-long supporter of the goals and campaigns of the Arts and Crafts Movement. Norton endeavoured to revive the Arts and Crafts spirit in Boston and throughout the United States.

ARTS AND CRAFTS EXHIBITIONS
Few who acknowledged the need for design reform could escape the compelling

Left: A cover for Deutsche Kunst und Dekoration [German Art and Decoration] *designed by Margaret Macdonald Mackintosh.*

Right: 'Michaelmas Daisy' wallpaper designed by Morris & Co and first produced in 1912.

Below: 'Medway' printed cotton (registered in 1885), created by Morris at Merton Abbey using the original indigo discharge system.

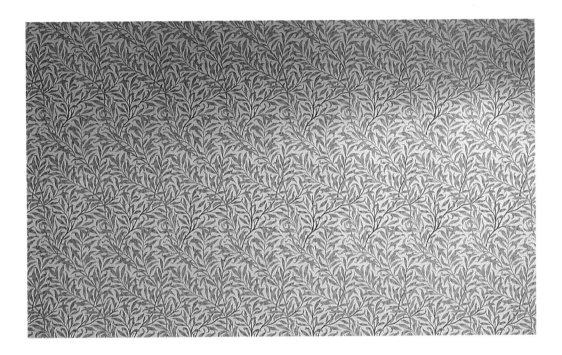

arguments of such writers as Norton, Pugin, Ruskin or Morris, whose works continued to inspire supporters into the second decade of the twentieth century. The challenge for their supporters lay first in translating their ideals into reality and then in convincing the public of the advantages offered by the products of the design-reform movement. One means was through public exhibitions of handicrafts, which were regularly held at local, regional and national levels, under the auspices of various design-reform organisations, and were dedicated to elevating the standards of public taste. Since most of them were competitions as well as exhibitions, they also raised the technical and aesthetic standards of the participants by stimulating a healthy professional rivalry.

WORLD FAIRS

World fairs provided an opportunity for international exposure, although their emphasis upon contemporary developments in machine technology seemed somewhat antithetical to the goals of the Arts and Crafts Movement. Initially, design reformers participated in these events in limited numbers. Morris, Marshall, Faulkner & Co, for example, was among the few to represent the cause at London's International Exhibition of 1862. But eventually numerous adherents began to take advantage of the fairs to promote their work. They contributed hundreds of noteworthy displays, for example, to the palaces of manufactures, varied industries and art at the Universal Exposition held in St Louis, Missouri, in 1904.

Above: 'Willow Boughs' wallpaper, designed by William Morris in 1887. Such a wallpaper emphasises the flatness of the wall and avoids a false illusion of depth.

Below: Metal baskets designed by Josef Hoffmann, the co-founder of the Wiener Werkstätte and a member of the Vienna Secession, c. 1905.

This exposition was proof of the widespread and growing acceptance of Arts and Crafts ideals, with exhibits from every part of Britain, most major cities in the United States and from many European countries, including Austria, Belgium, Denmark, France, Germany, The Netherlands, Italy and Sweden. Together with those from Canada, the Far East and South America, they demonstrated that the Anglo-American movement for design reform had become international in scope.

THE DISSEMINATION OF THE IDEAL

The acceptance of the movement outside Britain can be attributed to a variety of other features. Its products and propaganda were featured in a growing number of periodicals with an international audience, including *The*

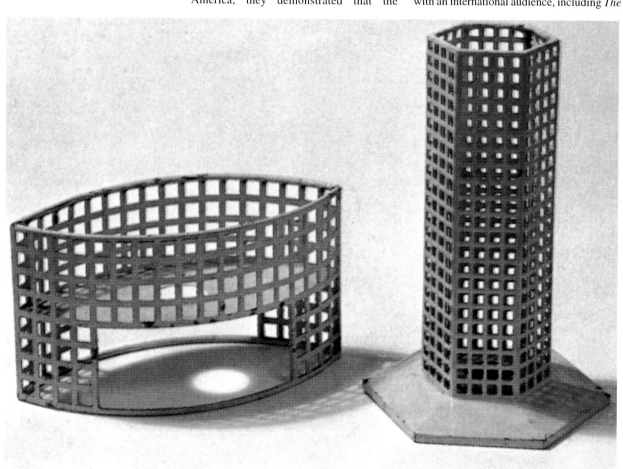

Studio, The Craftsman, Arte Italiana Decorativa ed Industriale, Art et Décoration, Dekorative Kunst and *Kunst und Handwerk,* as well as in such influential books as *Das Englische Haus [The English House],* written by the German architect Hermann Muthesius.

The cause was the focus of international lecture tours during the last decades of the nineteenth century by such leading figures as Christopher Dresser, Oscar Wilde, Walter Crane and C R Ashbee. Its attitude and approach were transmitted through travel or study abroad and through the interchange between nation and nation of skilled designers and craftsmen. Imported and domestic examples of 'art produce' were sold at an increasing pace in retail stores, which ranged from sales rooms associated with Arts and Crafts guilds or societies to mail-order concerns, speciality shops and department stores (the most

Below: A box made of various woods designed by Koloman Moser, the co-founder with Hoffmann of the Wiener Werkstätte, c. 1905.

Above: A silver-gilt tea service designed by Josef Hoffmann in 1904.

influential being the London enterprise founded in 1875 by Arthur Lasenby Liberty).

EUROPEAN GUILDS

While all of these played a part in furthering the Arts and Crafts ideal, the most effective means of dissemination remained the guild or society, based on British or American examples. Many organisations dedicated to design reform were established throughout Europe at the turn of the century, among them the Austrian Wiener Werkstätte and German Werkbund groups, and societies such as the Dansk Kunstfudforening (Danish Society for Industrial Arts) and the Svenska Slojdsforeningen (Swedish Society of Industrial Arts).

THE WIENER WERKSTÄTTE

Founded in Vienna in 1903 by Josef Hoffmann and Koloman Moser, and financed by Fritz Wärndorfer and Otto Primavesi, the Werkstätte were influenced by the example of Ashbee in England and the many craft workshops that were springing up in Germany, and also claimed kinship with Ruskin and Morris. In their Werkstätte manifesto, Hoffmann and Moser made no distinction between the fine and applied arts and stressed that the design of objects should reflect the innate qualities of the materials from which they were made. These principles were applied to virtually all conceivable fields, from architecture and

Right: 'Holland Park'-design Hammersmith carpet. This design was first produced for the home of A Ionides at 1 Little Holland Park in 1883; Morris used it again for this carpet, made in about 1886–89, for Clouds, the country house of the Honorable Percy Wyndham.

interior design to fashion and cutlery, all of which were to be co-ordinated to reflect a distinctly modern spirit.

The Werkstätte maintained a very high public profile in both national and international exhibitions in Vienna, Rome, Cologne and Paris, and stores selling Werkstätte products were located not only in fashionable quarters of Vienna, but also in Germany, Switzerland and the United States.

The Werkstätte were ambivalent in their attitude to industry, vacillating between a respect for the handcrafted and the realisation that no contemporary design workshop could ignore the increasing trend towards industrialisation. A high respect for craftsmanship and the creative autonomy of its designers, a strong antipathy against poorly designed and mass-produced goods, and

funding from wealthy patrons did little to help the Werkstätte face up to the harsher side of the business world. In practice, the workshops' ideals proved contradictory.

THE UNION OF ART AND INDUSTRY

Although the European guilds differed in structure and membership, all promoted high standards of design and craftsmanship and artistic co-operation. In doing so, they not only continued the campaign that had been launched by Pugin, Ruskin and Morris, but also anticipated the union of art and industry that was to become the focus of design reformers during the twentieth century. In focusing on textiles and interiors, this book examines two of the main areas in which Arts and Crafts ideals were successfully harnessed to industrial practices.

Below: 'Bachelor's Button' wallpaper, designed by William Morris in 1892, one of his few late wallpapers.

BRITISH TEXTILES AND INTERIORS

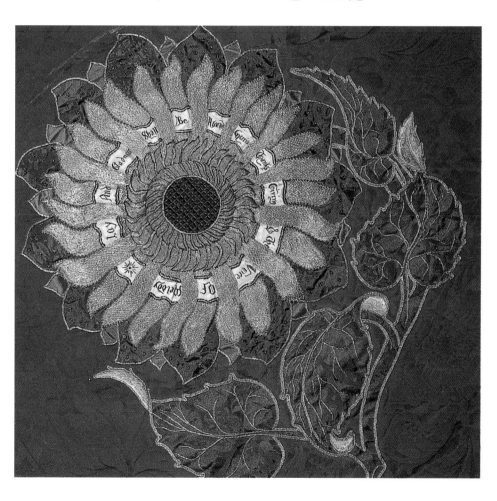

Previous page: An embroidered piano cover by C R Ashbee and the Guild and School of Handicraft.

Below: William Morris, photographed dressed in a hat and smock for work in the dye house.

Right: 'Flowerpot' printed cotton, indigo discharged, designed by Morris and registered in 1883.

In an essay on art and crafts, William Morris wrote: 'The special limitations of the material should be a pleasure to you, not a hindrance: a designer, therefore, should always thoroughly understand the process of the special manufacture he is dealing with, or the result will be a mere *tour de force*'.

Nowhere did he himself apply this dictum more stringently than in his work with textiles. As in other fields, he wanted not only to recreate the beauty of medieval examples, but to recreate them under working conditions that would gratify their makers.

THE QUEST FOR AUTHENTIC COLOUR
He soon realised, however, that the enduring colour qualities that he admired in such historic textiles as the tapestries in great European cathedrals could not be achieved with commercial synthetic dyes. He therefore set about reviving the ancient techniques of vegetable dyeing, conducting his earliest experiments in 1865 on wool and silk embroidery yarns at the premises of Morris, Marshall, Faulkner & Co in Queen Square, London. These were, however, limited in scope, and in order to delve more deeply into the art he enlisted the aid of Thomas Wardle, a silk dyer and printer from Leek in Staffordshire. Their chief sources included early references, such as John Gerard's *Herball* of 1597 and 1636, as well as contemporary practical manuals, of which *L'impression des Tissus*, by Persoz, published in Paris in 1846, appears to have been the most useful. But it was not until 1881, when the firm acquired the Merton Abbey Tapestry Works, that he began to achieve truly successful dyes.

MERTON ABBEY
The tapestry works, which had been built in the eighteenth century as silk-weaving sheds

and were taken over by textile printers in the nineteenth century, were well located on the banks of the river Wandle, which provided a constant water supply. Here Morris installed the dye vats which enabled him to reinstate the ancient technique of indigo discharge

printing. Indigo, along with woad, had been used for centuries to create deep and lasting blues, but the pigment could not be printed directly since it oxidised on contact with the air. The fabric had therefore to be dyed and the pattern afterwards discharged – or erased

Below: 'Evenlode' printed cotton, indigo discharged, designed by Morris and registered in 1883, the first of the Morris designs to be named after a tributary of the Thames.

Below: A painting of the pond at Merton Abbey by Lexdon Lewis Peacock (1850–1919). The Firm moved to this idyllic setting on the banks of the River Wandle in Surrey in 1881.

– with a bleaching agent. This laborious process had been superseded for commercial printing by the introduction of the mineral Prussian-blue dye towards the end of the eighteenth century.

Morris, using the original indigo-discharge system, created some of his most memorable narrative designs, among them 'Brer Rabbit', 'Bird and Anemone' and 'Strawberry Thief',

for which Philip Webb is believed to have drawn the birds. 'Strawberry Thief' is one of several where additional colours were added by overprinting.

BLOCK-PRINTING

For all of these, as for his other Merton Abbey printed textiles, Morris used hand-block-printing, the commercial application of which

Below: A painting of the pond at Merton Abbey by Lexdon Lewis Peacock (1850–1919). The Firm moved to this idyllic setting on the banks of the River Wandle in Surrey in 1881.

had fallen off considerably by the late nineteenth century, although it was still retained for some wallpaper and high-class furnishing and dress prints. The new and faster method of continuous printing using engraved-cylinder machines had largely taken over.

Block-printing held many attractions for Morris. It provided job satisfaction for the worker, offered no limitations to the colour and scale of designs, and provided him with scope for further experiments in discharge printing. On the negative side were the comparative slowness and the high cost. Although neither deterred Morris, they did mean that the fabrics were too expensive for anyone except the relatively rich. With this venture, nevertheless, he breathed new life into

Left: 'Brer Rabbit' printed cotton, designed by Morris and registered in 1882. The name of this design refers to the Uncle Remus stories, which Morris and his children enjoyed.

Below: 'Strawberry Thief' printed cotton, indigo discharged, designed by Morris and registered in 1883.

Right: 'Wild Tulip' wallpaper by William Morris, 1884. Here, and in later papers, Morris makes extensive use of dots, produced by driving metal pins into the wood block, as shading on leaves and as background.

an old craft and paved the way for further developments in the twentieth century.

MORRIS' PATTERN DESIGNS

His pattern designs both for textiles and wallpapers had a more immediate impact on the retail trade. From the *naïveté* of such early wallpaper designs as 'Daisy', 'Trellis' and 'Fruit' (also known as 'Pomegranate'), he soon advanced to the sophisticated complexity of overlaying 'nets', or diapers, and diagonal 'branches'. These were often inspired by historic textiles, particularly Indian, Turkish, Persian and Italian. The Italian silk-cut velvets acquired by London's South Kensington (now Victoria and Albert) Museum in 1883, for instance, have long been associated with such later print designs as 'Wey', 'Wandle' and 'Kennet'. Morris' woven textiles reflected the same sources.

WEAVING

Morris' involvement with weaving came later and brought him less personal gratification. Having mastered the principles by practising with a toy hand loom, he acknowledged that the mechanical Jacquard loom could achieve the desired effects. Somewhat surprisingly, he regarded this method as an acceptable variant on hand-loom weaving. He had sufficient technical knowledge to produce the point papers which guided the weavers, who were, for the most part, outside contractors.

Historical models were, again, the chief sources for Morris' designs in weaving. Mythical beasts, birds and dragons frequently appear, as do the familiar 'turnover', or mirror-image, effects. Some of his designs were adapted directly from medieval Italian brocades and Spanish silks. His carpets, in turn, reveal strong links with their Eastern heritage.

CARPETS

Morris was more practical – realistic, in terms of public needs and public purses – in his carpet production than in any of his other endeavours. He was less insistent on historical precedent for the general market, even going as far as to create one pattern, a composition of repeating African marigolds, that was produced on linoleum, as well as a number of striking designs for manufacture by machine. His most respected carpets, however, were hand-knotted, employing traditional techniques of the ancient oriental carpets of which he was both a student and a collector. In his own homes, he used them more often as wall hangings than as floor coverings.

He by no means intended to copy, writing in a Morris & Co brochure: 'We people of the West must make our own hand-made Carpets if we are to have any worth the labour and money such things cost: and that these, while they should equal the Eastern ones as nearly as may be in material and durability, should by no means imitate them in design, but show themselves obviously to be the outcome of modern Western ideas'. He and J H Dearle designed almost all of the carpets that were hand-knotted at Merton Abbey.

Above right: 'Fruit', also known as 'Pomegranate', wallpaper by William Morris, 1864. One of the first three wallpapers designed by Morris, it did not sell well.

Right: 'Bird' woven-wool double cloth, designed by William Morris in 1878 for the drawing room at Kelmscott House.

Below: A design for a rug by William Morris. Morris drew his carpet designs about one-eighth of the full size.

Below right: 'Marigold' printed cotton by William Morris. It was first used as a wallpaper and was registered as a textile design in 1875.

MORRIS' TAPESTRIES

For Morris, tapestry constituted 'the noblest of the weaving arts'. Since it could be produced only by hand, it remained for him the most philosophically and technically linked to its medieval roots. Although his deep admiration for tapestry stemmed from his formative visits to France in the 1850s with Edward Burne-Jones, it was not until 1879 that he set up his first experimental loom in his bedroom at Kelmscott House, where he taught himself to weave with the help of eighteenth-century French manuals. After three months he produced a stunningly intricate panel, 'Acanthus and Vine' – more affectionately known as 'Cabbage and Vine' because of 'the leaves' unruliness'. It employed the 'turnover' device, which he had already used to good effect in his woven designs.

This success led him to establish a loom at Queen Square, where he took on J H Dearle as an apprentice, who was to become one of the firm's leading designers in all its many disciplines. Dearle subsequently trained others in the high-warp, or vertical, tapestry technique which Morris used, and which differed considerably from the horizontal, low-warp method of the only existing English producer, the Royal Windsor Tapestry Works. Production began on a large scale with the move to Merton

Abbey in 1881, where three looms could be accommodated, with as many as three weavers each working at at time, and capable of producing huge, wall-sized tapestries.

The designs came mostly from Morris and Burne-Jones. The latter was responsible for virtually all of the Pre-Raphaelite figures, some of which were originally intended for stained glass. Morris designed only three complete tapestries but provided much of the decorative detail for Burne-Jones' figures. Dearle also supplied background foliage and eventually complete schemes.

Morris' involvement stimulated a revival

Below left: 'Lily' Wilton pile carpet, designed by William Morris in about 1875. It was one of the most popular of Morris' designs for machine-made carpets.

Below right: 'Acanthus and Vine', Morris'
first tapestry, which he called 'Cabbage
and Vine' because of the difficulty which he
had with the acanthus leaves. It was woven
in about four months in 1879 on the loom
which Morris set up in his bedroom at
Kelmscott House.

in tapestry production in Britain for a century. The Dovecot Studios, founded as the Edinburgh Tapestry Weaving Company in 1912 with weavers trained at Merton Abbey, was a direct outgrowth. The Merton Abbey Tapestry Works continued to produce for private houses, churches and other large public places until World War II.

BRITISH EMBROIDERY

In Britain, the standard of embroidery had declined both technically and artistically by the middle of the nineteenth century. Originality had been discouraged a century earlier with the appearance of printed charts

and patterns and had by now been almost obliterated by the popularity of Berlin woolwork. The influence of Pugin, among others, had brought about a dramatic upgrading in church embroidery from the 1840s.

MORRIS' EMBROIDERIES

The architect G E Street, in whose office Morris was briefly articled during 1856, had been a prime mover in this renaissance. Street, a confirmed medievalist, undoubtedly helped to shape the young man's ideas about the ancient art. Certainly, embroidery was the first textile technique with which Morris became personally involved. He studied early English

medieval ecclesiastical embroideries – *opus angelicanum* – but in his own early attempts he appears to have used wool yarn couched, or laid, on woollen fabric rather than the metal threads associated with ecclesiastical work.

His first known embroidery, repeatedly incorporating the words 'If I can', was worked in aniline-dyed crewel wools with irregular long and short stitches, which created a heavy, tapestry-like piece. Having accomplished this, Morris embroidered no more, but, acting as teacher, passed the production on to others. He designed several friezes and panels for Red House, which were embroidered by his wife, Jane, and her sister, Elizabeth Burden. With the founding of Morris, Marshall, Faulkner & Co in 1861, both domestic and ecclesiastical embroideries were undertaken, with the firm's participating members all contributing designs and the work being performed only with yarns dyed to their specifications in their own premises.

MAY MORRIS AND THE ROYAL SCHOOL OF ART NEEDLEWORK

In 1885, Morris' daughter, May, took control of the embroidery section. A skilled craftswoman, she herself became an influential figure, the author of definitive book, *Decorative Needlework*, and a teacher in major

Above left: 'The Adoration of the Magi', a tapestry designed by Edward Burne-Jones in 1887 and woven by Morris & Co in 1890.

Left: 'Love Leading the Pilgrim', a tapestry by William Morris and Edward Burne-Jones.

Below right: 'Vine' embroidered hanging, designed by Morris and worked by May Morris and her assistants in around 1890.

Arts and Crafts schools, both in Britain and in the United States. These included the prestigious Royal School of Art Needlework in London, for which Morris and Burne-Jones had produced designs in its fledgling days.

Founded in 1872 under the patronage of Queen Victoria's daughter, Princess Christian of Schleswig-Holstein, the school was dedicated to the restoration of 'Ornamental Needlework for secular purposes to the high place it once held among decorative arts'. It provided training and employment for educated young women and encouraged them to reproduce the best examples of old English needlework. Its goal was the perfection of practical skills rather than of creativity, which seems an ironic contradiction of Arts and Crafts ideals. Designs were provided in the form of sketches by leading artists and designers – Selwyn Image, G F Bodley, Walter Crane – some, including Morris patterns, are still available today.

OTHER EMBROIDERY SOCIETIES

Other, similar organisations grew up elsewhere. The Leek Embroidery Society, in Staffordshire, was established in 1879 by Elizabeth Wardle, the wife of the silk weaver Thomas Wardle, who had helped Morris with his early dyeing experiments. The society gained a reputation for ecclesiastical work, heavily applying silk and gold threads to plain

and printed tussore silk, brocades, velvets and velveteens. It also used Thomas Wardle's silks, some of which had been printed with William Morris' designs.

In the south of England, at Haslemere, Surrey, Godfrey Blount established in 1896 the Peasant Art Society as part of a working community of artists and craftspeople, known as Peasant Industries, which looked to peasant crafts as a source of design. The society created hangings made of hand-woven linen, vegetable-dyed and appliquéd. With flat, unshaded areas and strong outlines, it achieved an effect that suggested stained-glass windows.

Liberty & Co, already known as a supplier of 'art fabrics', was also instrumental in reinstating embroidery as a creative activity. The opening of its costume department in 1884 reinforced the importance of historical models as a source of visual and practical reference. Traditional crafts were also influential, and smocking became a speciality.

SCOTTISH EMBROIDERY

In Scotland, new ideas in embroidery were disseminated through educational institutions and exhibitions, the major contributors and innovators being women. Phoebe Traquair, one of the most talented, was skilled as a muralist, bookbinder and enameller, as well as an

Below left: A hanging (detail) worked in silk on linen by Ann Macbeth, Glasgow, Scotland, c. 1900. This early piece shows how appliqué was developed to significant effect by Macbeth, following the example of Jessie Newbery.

Below: An artists' view of the Royal School of Art Needlework's workroom in 1904.

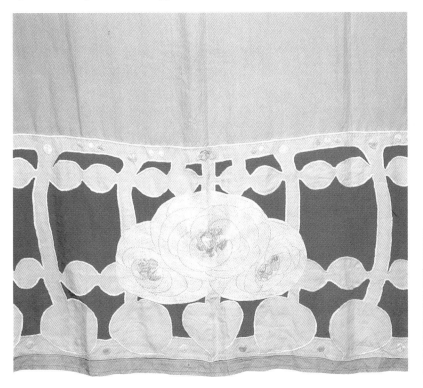

Below: An embroidery attributed to Anne Knox-Arthur, Glasgow, Scotland, c. 1900–10. The delicate colours and abstract motifs worked on coarse fabric are characteristic of the Glasgow style.

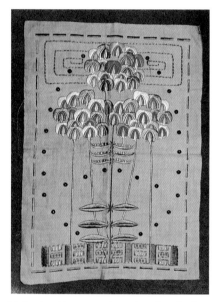

Right: A table runner in embroidered silk and linen, with appliqué cotton and cotton braid, attributed to Charles Rennie Mackintosh, Glasglow, Scotland, c. 1900–6/ This piece was worked by Margaret Macdonald Mackintosh.

embroiderer. Her most ambitious piece of needlework, the 'Denys' series, consisted of four screens depicting allegorical figures and was extravagantly wrought in gold and silk thread on linen. This was displayed by the Arts and Crafts Exhibition Society in 1903, and other pieces of her work were exhibited regularly in Europe and the United States.

At the same time, the Glasgow School of Art was becoming a focus for a special form of creative activity in which art embroidery played a pronounced role. Leadership came first from Jessie Newbery, a teacher at the school, and later from three of her students: the Macdonald sisters, Frances and Margaret, and especially Ann Macbeth, who produced needlework in what became known as the 'Glasgow style'. This evolved by way of the techniques developed by Morris and the Royal School of Art Needlework into something distinctive and recognisable, involving the use of appliqué, minimal amounts of stitching and needle-weaving on homely fabrics such as hessian, unbleached calico, flannel and linen. The purposes were practical – cushion covers, bags, belts, collars – and individual creativity

was encouraged. The decorative techniques were bold and simple, but they were wrought with perfection.

The style was characterised by soft tones of silver, pearl grey, pink and lilac, usually set off by heavily embroidered lines and often including lettering. The motifs were more conventionalised than those typically associated with the Arts and Crafts Movement. Florals and vegetation were common features and the stylised 'Glasgow rose', which was probably invented by Jessie Newbery, appeared frequently.

BRITISH TEXTILE MANUFACTURERS

Despite his innovative involvement in the craft of textile manufacture, Morris had little effect on either the production methods or the structure of the textile industry. The basic design vocabulary remained constant: florals still predominated in chintzes, with the occasional addition of animals, birds and figures. However, the patterns that Morris introduced did lead to an entirely new treatment of these traditional forms. During the 1880s and 1890s, the previously conventional patterns

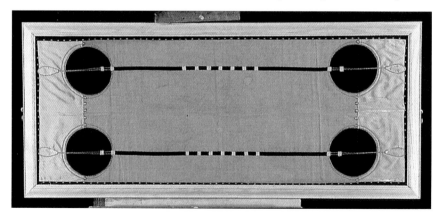

THIS·YERE·THE·LEAF·OR·THE·FLOWER·

of furnishing textiles and wallpaper became increasingly stylised, contributing profoundly to the development of Art Nouveau. And designers were becoming known as individuals. Manufacturers of British textiles had, in the past, insisted on anonymity, but by the end of the century they were revealing – even advertising – their designers' names. The example had been set by the Arts and Crafts Exhibition Society, which displayed both the name of the manufacturer and of the designer beside exhibits.

DAY, CRANE AND VOYSEY
In the commercial textile trade, the patterns of Lewis F Day, Walter Crane and C F A Voysey had particular impact. In 1881 Day was appointed art director of the Lancashire textile printers Turnbull and Stockdale. Although his floral designs for them often seem formal and derivative, they were important in conveying the new style to a wide public. Crane's patterns, by contrast, reveal a well-developed skill in portraying birds, animals and the human form. He, too, designed a range of textiles and wrote and lectured about ornament and design. Both men also created wallpaper patterns for Jeffrey & Co, the high-class London hand-block printers. Voysey's work was more original than that of the other two. He produced a vast number of textile and wallpaper designs, all reflecting his conviction that simplicity in decoration should be recognised as a source of richness. Initial reference to historical patterns developed into clear, flat colours, combined with florals, naïve figures and birds. Unlike Morris, none of these men was involved in the production process, but they were dependent on the patronage of enlightened manufacturers to convey their designs to the public.

Left: 'La Margarete' wallpaper panel by Walter Crane.

*Below right: Wallpaper frieze by Rex Silver,
produced by John Line & Sons, London,
c. 1905. The stylised, linear motifs, typical
of the Silver Studio's work between 1900
and 1910, replaced the full-blown Art
Nouveau of the late 1890s and influenced
the development of French decorative art in
the early 1920s. John Line & Sons was a
major hand and machine wallpaper printer.*

LIBERTY & CO AND SILVER STUDIO

Retailers also played a significant role in the process of dissemination, the leader among them being Liberty & Co of London. In all of the many ways in which the shop translated the Arts and Crafts ideal into commercial reality none was more far-reaching than its participation in this field of textiles.

Many of Liberty's most characteristic fabrics, including its famous 'Peacock Feather', originated in the remarkable, London-based Silver Studio, which supplied the shop continuously until World War II. Founded in 1880 by the fabric designer Arthur Silver, it was subsequently run by his two sons, Rex and Harry. Historic textiles provided the basis for many of their patterns and Arthur, a keen amateur photographer, produced a unique photographic record of historic textiles in the Victoria and Albert Museum which were sold throughout the 1890s to progressive manufacturers. The studio was frequently required to adapt Morris patterns for machine production, which helped to bring knowledge of his designs, if not his philosophy, to the cheaper end of the market. By the turn of the century, two Silver Studio designers, Harry Napper and John Ilingworth Kay, were providing a strong stylistic impetus for Art Nouveau. Silver Studio designs were sold to manufacturers in the United States and Europe, as well as in Britain, the style-conscious French being among the most enthusiastic purchasers.

EUROPEAN AND AMERICAN TEXTILES AND INTERIORS

The reverberations of the British Arts and Crafts Movement continued to resonate strongly elsewhere in the world, but almost everywhere it was usually distinguished by a strong national identification rather than displaying a homogenous style.

DECORATIVE MOTIFS

The provincial sympathies of Arts and Crafts designers were exemplified by the decorative motifs found on surfaces, textiles, furnishings and objects: many were of humble origin, associated for generations with the folk tradition. The decorative vocabulary consisted of simple, geometrical shapes and conventionalised natural motifs, used individually or as repetitive patterns or borders. Popular devices included the tulip, rose, leaf and bird. But chief among these was the heart, which appeared on forms as diverse as leaded glass by the American designer Will Bradley, cupboards by the British designer Charles Rennie Mackintosh, chair backs by C F A Voysey and firedogs by Ernest Gimson.

Justifications for the popularity of these folk motifs were at least threefold. Firstly, they were compatible stylistically with the provincial nature of many Arts and Crafts designs. Secondly, they were as simple and direct in form as were the shapes and surfaces that they embellished. And thirdly, they evoked the positive, homely virtues that design reformers hoped to restore to daily life. But they were

Previous page: Portière *by George W Mahler and Louis J Millet, USA, 1901. Made in cotton and silk velvet, the design was appliquéd in cotton damask and embroidered in silk.*

Left: 'Medway' printed cotton, indigo discharged, by Morris, registered in 1885.

by no means used in a simplistic fashion: rather, they were manipulated in a sophisticated manner which belied their humble origins. In the hands of an accomplished designer, they assumed an air of calculated *naïveté*.

Equally sophisticated were the patterns that were derived from natural sources and were often regional in their character. Morris' distinctive chintzes, wallpapers and carpets immortalised the wild flowers and vegetation growing along streams and in country gardens in south-eastern England. Mackintosh's sinuous wall stencils and embroideries provided variations upon the traditional Glasgow rose, which flourishes in Scotland's grey, damp climate. Frank Lloyd Wright's stained-glass windows, lighting fixtures and carpets captured with angular precision the essence of weeds, seed pods and trees growing wild on the prairies of the American Midwest. And Candace Wheeler's appliqués and tapestries transformed in subtle tone-on-tone the thistles, pine cones, ivy and shells of the north-eastern United States. All of these had a freshness and originality that resulted from a close observation of nature. But, by virtue of colour, composition, scale and modelling, they were transformed from the commonplace into the extraordinary.

THE USE OF COLOUR

Colour, as one component of beauty, was treated variously by Arts and Crafts architects and designers. The British designers Voysey

Right: Library, Glasgow School of Art, Glasgow, Scotland, 1877–99, 1907–9, Charles Rennie Mackintosh. The interior expresses a quest for verticality and light in the manner of the Gothic.

Below: 'Brita's Forty Winks, illustration for Ett Hem, *by the Swedish painter Carl Larsson, 1899.*

and M H Baillie Scott, as well as the Swede Carl Larsson and the American Will Bradley, included large blocks of vivid colour to define interior planes boldly. Others, such as Mackintosh or the Viennese Josef Hoffmann, utilised an achromatic palette of whites, greys and blacks enlivened with strategic touches of brilliant colour. Another group offered a conservative approach: Philip Webb, Edward Ould, Stanford White and Henry Hobson Richardson incorporated chintzes, wallpapers or oriental rugs as subtle, multi-coloured accents. The majority, however, eliminated bright colour altogether, choosing instead to emphasise the dull tones of structural materials, such as wood, stone, brick, plaster, metal or leather.

TEXTILES

Like colour, textiles were partially responsible for the usefulness and beauty of an Arts and Crafts interior. In some interiors, every form was padded and every surface draped, while in later interiors and those designed by architects, fabric and cushioning were kept to a minimum. The relative presence or absence of those elements affected profoundly the overall character of the room.

Left: A love seat by John Henry Belter

In some Arts and Crafts interiors, textiles were utilised as they had been throughout the nineteenth century. Comfortable seating pieces displayed buttons, tufts and trims, while draperies hung at the windows. Tapestries lined walls above the dado and patterned rugs covered the floor. Lambrequins adorned mantels, and cloths extended from table top to floor. As a result, the features of the room and frames of seat furniture were obscured rather than exposed. Textiles used in so generous a manner were particularly evident in Arts and Crafts interiors in England, Scandinavia and the United States. They were especially prominent in interiors furnished by enterprises having a vested interest in their use, such as Morris & Co, Liberty & Co and Associated Artists.

What distinguished these draped and upholstered interiors as products of the Arts and Crafts Movement were the woven or printed patterns that they contained. The patterns were modelled subtly and appeared relatively flat to emphasise the flatness of the planes which they covered. They tended to be stylised and carefully composed, in contrast to the undulating, naturalistic patterns of the Victorian age. Such stylisation discouraged the impression conveyed by large-scale, realistic patterns – that the user was sitting or walking upon living specimens of flowers or foliage.

THE INFLUENCE OF OTHER STYLES

During the life span of the Arts and Crafts Movement, this varied approach to the use of colour and textiles reflected the influence of other styles and movements then in vogue.

Right: A hand-woven carpet by Eliel Saarinen, Finland, 1904.

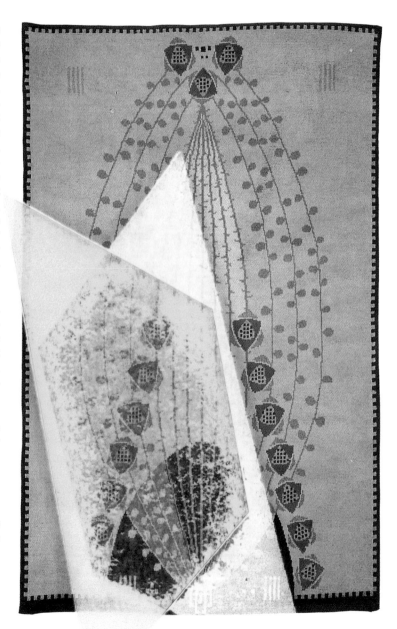

Some had little impact on Arts and Crafts interiors, while others affected everything from colour and texture to form and motif to broader issues of planning and arrangement. Among these were the Gothic Revival and High Victorian Gothic styles, the Old English, Queen Anne, Colonial and Georgian revivals, as well as national Romanticism and the English Domestic Revival Movement.

SCANDINAVIAN TEXTILES

In Scandinavia, guilds and societies along Morrisian lines were formed to preserve traditional craft skills and to stimulate fresh interpretations of them. Schools of arts and crafts were opened in Stockholm, Sweden, and in Helsinki, Finland, and the public was encouraged to open weaving studios and to create work of its own. Design inspiration came initially from folk patterns, but the reawakened artistic spirit soon led to the emergence of new forms. In Finland, Axel Gallen-Kallela employed brilliant, flame-like motifs in his textiles. He produced as bed covers hand-knotted, shaggy-pile *ryijy* rugs of the type originally made by peasants to put on the floor. Gabriel Engberg also contributed decisively to the revival of the *ryijy* with her use of bold geometrics.

NORWEGIAN TEXTILES

Following the lead given by the Paris Exposition Universelle of 1900, which demonstrated how effectively influences from abroad could be united with native

Left: Variation II, *by the German artist Paul Klee, 1924. Klee contributed to the work of the Bauhaus' stained-glass and weaving workshops.*

techniques, the Norwegians turned to eighteenth-century tapestries for a lead. They coupled stylised biblical motifs with the heroic dragon found in their own Norse legends to achieve striking results. This fusion can be seen most markedly in the work of the Impressionist painter Gerard Munthe, who led a tapestry revival that parallels William Morris' activities at Merton Abbey. He developed advanced ideas on the use of stylisation, which he put into practice in a long series of cartoons derived from folklore subjects. The tapestries were then made up by professional weavers. Munthe's 'The Three Suitors', woven for the 1900 Paris Exhibition, for example, reveals the successful amalgamation of medieval tradition that Munthe achieved with his own, contemporarily flattened, linear style.

Frida Hansen, another of Norway's most important designers and weavers, was also initially influenced by a combination of tradition and the new styles that she encountered on a visit to Paris in 1895. In 1897 she founded the Norwegian Tapestry weaving studio in Oslo, where she devised a method of 'transparent' weaving, in which areas of the warp were left exposed to contrast with large, stylised floral motifs in bright colours.

Left: A woven-silk tapestry made by Anni Albers at the Bauhaus weaving workshop in 1926.

Opposite page: Slit gobelin with linen warp and cotton woof, woven in the weaving workshops of the Dessau Bauhaus by Gunta Stölzl, 1927–28.

Below: A cotton carpet designed for a nursery by Benita Otte at the Bauhaus, 1923.

SWEDISH TEXTILES

In Sweden, the Friends of Textile Art Association (Handarbetetsvanner) was founded to give women independence and to revive old textile techniques. The Swedish craft heritage was re-examined under the influence of the writings of Morris and Walter Crane. New designs were devised which enhanced old techniques, and craft and home *slojd* exhibitions were held throughout the country.

EASTERN EUROPEAN TEXTILES

A similar arts and crafts reawakening was taking place in Eastern Europe, with traditional folk-art techniques providing sources for

woven textiles and lace. In Hungary, geometrical folk weaves revealed a combination of peasant art with a distinguishable and unique Scandinavian influence.

In Czechoslovakia, the painter, designer and weaver Rudolf Schlattauer founded a tapestry factory which aroused nationwide interest in textile art. This was evidenced in the relocation of Slovak arts and crafts from rural, peasant villages to professional, urban centres. Polish tapestry-weaving remained a part of that country's folk culture until the early twentieth century, when it also became subject to a more professional approach.

Cottage industries also persisted in Russia, especially in more remote areas. Women spun, wove and vegetable-dyed linen and wool for garments, which they embellished with drawn-threadwork and other forms of embroidery, using designs handed down through the generations. These were gradually taken up by Moscow artists, such as Nathalie Davidoff and Victor Vasnietzoff, who wanted to help to preserve the village crafts. They, in turn, designed embroideries for execution by peasant women, often based on local legends and fairy tales. Even here, there were marked Arts and Crafts overtones. Ruskin and Morris had made their mark.

GERMAN TEXTILES

The Deutscher Werkbund, a confraternity of craftsmen, architects and industrialists, was formed in 1907 from a number of *Werkstätte* (workshops) dedicated to the reform of the applied arts. The Werkbund went from strength to strength, with almost 2,000 members by the beginning of 1914. Its progress was, however, interrupted by the outbreak of World War I. Following in its tradition, the Bauhaus served as one of the last significant

Left: The drawing room at Mark Twain's house, Hartford, Connecticut, by Associated Artists. The textiles, wallpaper and carpets show how Associated Artists successfully developed its own Arts and Crafts style of interior decoration from historical influences to create an atmosphere of restrained elegance.

Below: A photograph of Candace Wheeler, one of the most prominent designers in the American Arts and Crafts Movement.

staging posts of the Arts and Crafts tradition. It was established in 1919 under the direction of Walter Gropius and had emerged from the amalgamated schools of fine and applied arts in Weimar. The programme of the Bauhaus contained a number of ideals common to the Arts and Crafts tradition, the prime point of departure being handicraft. It moved to Dessau in 1925 and closed in 1933.

Weaving, and later wallpapers, were two of the most commercially successful fields of Bauhaus production. One of the principal departures of the Bauhaus weaving style was its rejection of the pictorial mode which had dominated late-nineteenth-century and Art Nouveau hangings, the majority of which were in traditional tapestry weave. Many of the Bauhaus weavings were designed under the influence of the artist Paul Klee, who took a particular interest in the workshop, but while these and other 'artist'-designed pieces show a strong individualism, they are all executed in abstract patterning.

The products of the weaving workshop can be divided into four groups – individual pieces, commissioned works, series designs made in quantity at the Bauhaus itself and, fourthly, prototypes for industrial mass production. The workshop was taken over by Gunta Stölzl in 1927 (she had been a Bauhaus student), followed by Anni Albers in 1931 and finally by Lilly Reich in 1932. These three, and other talented designers, including Lies Dienhardt,

Right: Candace Wheeler, portrayed in this marble bas-relief by L Thompson, was an enthusiastic force in the American revival of embroidery as an art form.

Martha Erps, Gertrud Hautschk, Ruth Hollos, Benita Otte and particularly Otti Berger, all produced splendid work. Firms which produced Bauhaus textiles included the Poly-textil Gesellschaft of Berlin and Pausa of Stuttgart. Wallpapers were produced by Rasch between 1930 and 1931.

THE UNITED STATES

In the United States, where needlework skills had languished after the Civil War, new impetus was provided by the display of London's Royal School of Art Needlework at the 1876 Philadelphia Centennial Exhibition. So impressed was Candace Wheeler, a

prosperous, artistically influential woman, that she was prompted in 1887 to found the New York Society of Decorative Art, which she envisaged as an 'American Kensington School', with the objective of providing women with the opportunity to produce high-quality work that would not only be valued by society but

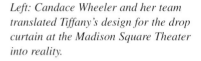

Left: Candace Wheeler and her team translated Tiffany's design for the drop curtain at the Madison Square Theater into reality.

would also be both recreational and profit-making. Its scope was wider than that of the Royal School of Art Needlework, but art needle-work was its chief focus. Englishwomen crossed the Atlantic to teach technique and design to this society, and to others which it generated in major American cities. Output included lace, ecclesiastical embroidery, hangings and tapestries, as well as sculpture, painting, wood-carving and pottery.

ASSOCIATED ARTISTS

Candace Wheeler herself moved dramatically into commerce when, in 1879, she entered into partnership with L C Tiffany to form Associated Artists, which rapidly became one of New York's leading interior-decorating firms. Also involved were the textile designer and colourist Samuel Colman and the orna-mental wood-carver Lockwood de Forest, who worked as a team from their Fourth Avenue atelier, much in the spirit of Morris & Co. They had planned to run a studio following the example of a Renaissance workshop, with Tiffany as the creative centre surrounded by assistants working in a variety of media, but ultimately the company had few parallels with Morris' experiment. The company worked mainly in the fields of glass and fabric design; its original purpose was ambitious: to estab-lish an alliance between art and industry and to revive the standards of domestic taste in the United States.

The textiles designed and produced by Associated Artists included luxurious curtains, *portières* and wall coverings, which made use of embroidery, needle-woven tapestry and loom weaving. The studios undertook commis-sions on the highest levels, from decorating the White House in Washington, DC, for President Chester Arthur, to creating opulent bed-hangings for the London home of Lillie

Below right: Samuel Colman, the water-colourist, was a collector of textiles. He travelled with Tiffany in the Middle East and both artists were fascinated by the designs that they saw. Tiffany was to build up a huge collection of oriental carpets. This sixteenth-century needlework carpet is from Turkey.

Langtry, which were embroidered in silk with 'sunset-coloured' roses. The company split early in the next decade, with Tiffany and Wheeler working independently, the one trading as Louis C Tiffany & Co and the other (Wheeler) as Associated Artists. Louis C Tiffany's work is well documented. Less well known, and more germane to the Arts and Crafts tradition in the United States, was the work of his associate, Candace Wheeler.

Candace Wheeler was the prime mover in initiating 'genuine' American designs, turning for inspiration to traditional patchwork, indigenous flora and fauna and events from American history and from literature. These were produced commercially for her by, among others, the Connecticut silk manufacturer Cheney Brothers. She was also personally involved with tapestries and patented a method of weaving in which a needle, rather than a shuttle, carried a soft weft across a durable silk canvas especially made for her by Cheney Brothers. Although the process was too costly to be financially viable, Associated Artists produced several major pieces, including 'The Miraculous Draught of Fishes', based on the Raphael cartoon in the Victoria and Albert Museum; and 'The Hiawatha Tapestry', based on Henry Wadsworth Longfellow's poem.

REVIVING INDIGENOUS TECHNIQUES

The last decades of the nineteenth century witnessed the formation of numerous American societies and schools which stimulated interest in textile arts and crafts and promoted the use of old techniques, such as netting and candlewick. Native American arts – particularly Navajo weaves – came to be prized and emulated for their striking patterns and simplicity of production on basic hand

looms. Similarly functional rag rugs, which had originally been made from used fabric, were now created from new materials, thus ensuring control of the designs.

By the turn of the twentieth century, however, the influence of the British Arts and Crafts Movement had subsided. The United States had succeeded in evolving original designs and techniques by looking at its own heritage. It should be noted, however, that the concepts of a 'national art' differed across the country. On the East Coast, Morrisian communities were founded, and furniture and other decorative items were made which had a direct resemblance to the British movement. In California, however, the climate and landscape,

and also the impact of the destruction of San Francisco in 1906, led to different interpretations. Morris' romantic return to the medieval European past was supplanted by the recognition of California's own past in Spanish-Mexican and Native American culture.

BREAKING THE BARRIERS

As in Britain, the Arts and Crafts Movement broke the barriers of traditional imitation in commercial areas such as wallpaper and fabric design and graphics. The adoption of Art Nouveau styles by firms such as the York Wallpaper Co or M H Birge & Sons allowed people to see for the first time that contemporary design was available.

Right: The dining room that Associated Artists designed for Mark Twain's house in Hartford, Connecticut.

ARTS AND CRAFTS MOVEMENT

TEXTILES AND INTERIORS

This book is due for return on or before the last date shown below.

1 0 MAY 2001

2 6 NOV 2003

2 6 NOV 2003

1 9 JAN 2007

0 1 FEB 2007

2 0 JAN 2009

1 0 MAR 2009